BASKETBALL LEGENDS

Kareem Abdul-Jabbar

Charles Barkley

Larry Bird

Wilt Chamberlain

Clyde Drexler

Julius Erving

Patrick Ewing

Anfernee Hardaway

Grant Hill

Magic Johnson

Michael Jordan

Jason Kidd

Reggie Miller

Hakeem Olajuwon

Shaquille O'Neal

Scottie Pippen

David Robinson

Dennis Rodman

CHELSEA HOUSE PUBLISHERS

DAVID ROBINSON

Hal Bock

Introduction by
Chuck Daly

CHELSEA HOUSE PUBLISHERS
Philadelphia

Produced by Daniel Bial and Associates
New York, New York

Picture research by Alan Gottlieb
Cover illustration by Bill Vann

First Printing

1 3 5 7 9 8 6 4 2

Library of Congress Cataloging-in-Publication Data

Bock, Hal.
    David Robinson / Hal Bock; introduction by Chuck Daly.
     p. cm. — (Basketball legends)
    Includes bibliographical references and index.
Summary: Discusses the life of David Robinson, star player for the San Antonio Spurs.
ISBN 0-7910-4387-8 (hardcover)
1. Robinson, David, 1965 –   —Juvenile literature. 2. Basketball players—United
States—Biography—Juvenile literature. 3. San Antonio Spurs (Basketball team)—
Juvenile literature. [1. Robinson, David, 1965 –   . 2. Basketball players. 3. Afro-
Americans—Biography.] I. Title. II. Series.
GV884.R615B63   1997
796.323'092—dc20
[B]   96-34637
                                                                                          CIP
                                                                                           AC

CONTENTS

BECOMING A BASKETBALL LEGEND

Chuck Daly

What does it take to be a basketball superstar? Two of the three things it takes are easy to spot. Any great athlete must have excellent skills and tremendous dedication. The third quality needed is much harder to define, or even put in words. Others call it leadership or desire to win, but I'm not sure that explains it fully. This third quality relates to the athlete's thinking process, a certain mentality and work ethic. One can coach athletic skills, and while few superstars need outside influence to help keep them dedicated, it is possible for a coach to offer some well-timed words in order to keep that athlete fully motivated. But a coach can do no more than appeal to a player's will to win; how much that player is then capable of ensuring victory is up to his own internal workings.

In recent times, we have been fortunate to have seen some of the best to play the game. Larry Bird, Magic Johnson, and Michael Jordan had all three components of superstardom in full measure. They brought their teams to numerous championships, and made the players around them better. (They also made their coaches look smart.)

I myself coached a player who belongs in that class, Isiah Thomas, who helped lead the Detroit Pistons to consecutive NBA crowns. Isiah is not tall-he's just over six feet-but he could do whatever he wanted with the ball. And what he wanted to do most was lead and win.

All the players I mentioned above and those whom this series will chronicle are tremendously gifted athletes, but for the most part, you can't play professional basketball at all unless you have excellent skills. And few players get to stay on their team unless they are willing to dedicate themselves to improving their talents even more, learning about their opponents, and finding a way to join with their teammates and win.

It's that third element that separates the good player from the superstar, the memorable players from the legends of the game. Superstars know when to take over the game. If the situation calls for a defensive stop, the superstars stand up and do it. If the situation calls for a key pass, they make it. And if the situation calls for a big shot, they want the ball. They don't want the ball simply because of their own glory or ego. Instead they know—and their teammates know—that they are the ones who can deliver, regardless of the pressure.

The words "legend" and "superstar" are often tossed around without real meaning. Taking a hard look at some of those who truly can be classified as "legends" can provide insight into the things that brought them to that level. All of them developed their legacy over numerous seasons of play, even if certain games will always stand out in the memories of those who saw them. Those games typically featured amazing feats of all-around play. No matter how great the fans thought the superstars were, these players were capable of surprising the fans, their opponents, and occasionally even themselves. The desire to win took over, and with their dedication and athletic skills already in place, they were capable of the most astonishing achievements.

CHUCK DALY, most recently the head coach of the New Jersey Nets, guided the Detroit Pistons to two straight NBA championships, in 1989 and 1990. He earned a gold medal as coach of the 1992 U.S. Olympic basketball team—the so-called "Dream Team"—and was inducted into the Pro Basketball Hall of Fame in 1994.

1
A SCORING CHAMPION

Each NBA regular season is more marathon than sprint, an 82-game endurance test that stretches from November until May and can become a blur of airports, hotel rooms and arenas, repeated night after night. So it is entirely understandable that when the San Antonio Spurs reached the final game of the 1993-94 season, there was a sense of relief among the players.

The Spurs had made an admirable run under Coach John Lucas but would not catch the Houston Rockets in the Midwest Division. They were locked into a second-place finish, no matter how the final game against the last-place Los Angeles Clippers came out.

Under ordinary circumstances, San Antonio might have been tempted to take it easy in order to prepare for the their first opponent in the playoffs, the Utah Jazz. These, however,

Despite being constantly double-teamed, David Robinson poured in 73 points against the Los Angeles Clippers to win the 1994 NBA scoring title.

were not ordinary circumstances. David Robinson, the team's franchise player, the guy around whom San Antonio's success was constructed, had plenty on the line that final Sunday of the season. He went into the last game with 2,312 points for the season, a 29.266 average, just a fraction of a point behind Orlando's Shaquille O'Neal, who had 2,345 points, a 29.313 average.

The NBA scoring championship had come down to the season's final day, Robinson playing an afternoon game at Los Angeles, O'Neal waiting to go that night in Orlando. So the Spurs would not have the leisure of relaxing in their last game. Instead, they were a team on a mission, determined to help Robinson win the scoring championship.

"We go to him every game but we'll do it even more on Sunday," guard Vinny Del Negro said. "We'd love to see him win that title."

Coach Lucas made it clear that Robinson's quest was vital to the Spurs. "We want to win the game," he said, "and we want David to get his points."

No problem there. Robinson went on a tear from the opening tap. Twenty seconds into the game, he nailed a jump shot and it was off to the races. He scored 18 points in the first quarter, all but two of San Antonio's total in those first 12 minutes. The Clippers were not amused at the one-man show and tried desperately to put a stop to it, often double- and triple-teaming Robinson.

In the second period, Robinson's drive for points hit a speed bump. He managed just six points. "I was kind of disappointed with only 24 at halftime," Robinson said. Spurs assistant coach George Gervin teased the 7'1" center. "He'd say, 'I had 53 in the first half,' " Robinson laughed.

Gervin had been down this road before. In 1977-78, the NBA scoring race went down to the last day as Gervin dueled Denver's David Thompson for the crown. Thompson, playing an afternoon game, scored 73 points. Gervin needed 58 that night to win the crown. He scored 53 in the first half and added another 10 in the third quarter. Having won the crown, he sat out the last period.

"I did what I had to do back then," Gervin said, "and David had to do what he had to do. I told him to take full advantage of the afternoon because he didn't want to look back with any regrets."

As Gervin sat down on the Spurs bench for the start of the third quarter, Robinson went back into overdrive, scoring 19 points. Now the 16,000 fans in the Los Angeles Sports Arena, including teammate Dennis Rodman's pal, Madonna, got swept up in the show and began cheering for Robinson every time down the floor. And every time, it seemed, Robinson responded with points.

He finished his day with 28 points in the fourth quarter, nailing a 17-footer on the baseline with 37 seconds left to close with 71 points.

In order to catch Robinson, O'Neal needed to amass 68 points that night against the Nets. He managed to score only 32, finishing with a 29.35 average to Robinson's 29.79. O'Neal and the Magic were not amused at the outcome of the league's closest scoring race since 1986.

"We certainly wanted Shaquille to win the scoring race," Magic coach Brian Hill said. "But we didn't want to make a mockery of the game the way they did in Los Angeles."

"I heard no defense was played," O'Neal said. "No triple teams occurred and they ran every play to him. If that would happen down here, I'd have 70 points, too."

That's where Shaq was wrong. Clippers coach Bob Weiss did not want his team playing the foil for Robinson. "We double-teamed him with our forwards every time we could," he said, "but he still scored the points. He was spectacular."

Robinson was all over the court against the Clippers, hitting jumpers inside and outside and once even knocking down a three-pointer from behind the arc.

He connected on 25 of 41 shots from the field, 1 for 2 on three-pointers and 18 for 25 from the foul line. "Obviously, I don't always take that many shots," Robinson said. "I've just never been that concerned with individual things. I want game wins."

The fact is, in the history of the NBA only three men — David Thompson in that last-day scoring title duel with Gervin, Elgin Baylor, now GM of the Clippers, and Wilt Chamberlain, who once scored 100 in a game — had topped 70 points.

Robinson was appropriately impressed with his day's work. "I looked up at the scoreboard and saw 71 points and said, 'My goodness, 71 points.' I just had to shake my head."

Rodman, who wrapped up the league rebounding title that day, thought Robinson could have

George Gervin won four NBA scoring titles as a member of the San Antonio Spurs between 1978 and 1982.

had more. "He missed a couple of free throws and a couple of easy baskets," he said. "But he deserves this."

Robinson politely denied O'Neal's suggestion that the Clippers had folded against him. "It was a lot of work going after those points," he said. "The Clippers didn't want me to get it. They were bumping and grinding and double-teaming me. That's the hardest I've ever had to work for some points.

"It was fun. I really had a good time."

Robinson's scoring explosion resulted in a 121-97 victory, a franchise record 55th win of the season — a mark the Spurs would break a year later when San Antonio had the best record in the league at 62-20.

Those are the numbers that matter most to Robinson. The points are nice. The wins are nicer. "As a leader, I just try to win games. That's my primary focus," said the scoring champ.

From the first day the Admiral (a nickname picked up from his days in the U.S. Navy) marched into the NBA, winning has been a tradition he established for San Antonio.

2
ANCHORS AWEIGH

Growing up, David Robinson was not exactly your average, run-of-the-mill student. In high school, he took advanced computer courses at a time when the internet and world wide web were still far in the future. In his spare time, he constructed a six-foot screen projection television set, just for something to do, then took it apart to show people how it worked, and put it back together again. When it was time to take the Scholastic Aptitude Test, Robinson scored a head-turning 1,320 out of a possible 1,600.

Average? Not in the classroom. On the basketball court, it was a far different story. There, Robinson did not exactly stand out. He was stringbean-sized at 6′6″ and 175 pounds and played just one year at Osbourne Park High School in Manassas, Virginia. He did not dazzle college basketball recruiters, but then with those SAT scores, he didn't have to.

When David Robinson was a kid he wanted to join the Navy.

Young David was developing into something of a Renaissance man. More than comfortable with academic subjects, he was an accomplished pianist who learned music from his father, and well-read, as well.

When it came time to select a college, Robinson never hesitated. He would attend the Naval Academy at Annapolis, not far from home in Manassas. He had Navy in his blood. His father, Ambrose, had just completed a 20-year hitch as a sonar technician. The Academy was nearby and provided more than enough of an intellectual challenge for someone with Robinson's ample academic ammunition.

With his credentials, Robinson could have gone anywhere. Had the Ivy League entered his thinking? "At an Ivy school, I would have had to play basketball," he said. "At Navy, I could take it or leave it.

"I went to the Academy because I wanted a great education. Basketball was secondary to me. I felt I had more academic potential than I showed in high school. I felt I needed a little discipline."

For that, he had come to the right place.

Robinson once described what it was like to go out on maneuvers at the Academy, running though the woods early in the morning, sometimes in the rain, sometimes with the temperature and humidity in a neck and neck race to see which hit 100 first. Your back hurts. Your feet hurt. Your head hurts.

It's about that time that the wills of some midshipmen are tested, that they wonder if maybe this Navy business wasn't such a good idea, after all.

David Robinson never wondered.

In a 1986 game against Fairfield University, Robinson set a Naval Academy record by snatching 25 rebounds. He also scored 19 points and blocked 8 shots.

Because of his size, he had gone out for the basketball team in his first year and was a non-factor, averaging 7.6 points and four rebounds a game. He missed the first four games because he had suffered a broken hand in a boxing class. In most places, you'd never see a basketball player get anywhere near a boxing ring. The Naval Academy, though, isn't just any place.

"With the emphasis on academics and the military, the Academy is a tough place to develop your game," Robinson said. "It's easy to get distracted from basketball. If you're not a great player with great potential, you might figure, 'Why waste my time?'

"The game didn't come naturally to me. I didn't play street ball, so I didn't have the moves, the intuitive stuff. I was getting my face beat up. And basketball was more work than fun. I knew I could prove myself academically, so I wanted to stick it out. I just wanted to play so I could get my letter."

After Robinson had become an NBA star, he reflected on those difficult early days of basketball at the Academy. "I remember when I first came into college, I remember that one of the first articles that someone wrote about me said that I looked like a swizzle stick in a blender playing. I think about that a lot and how far I've had to come from that time."

Robinson stood 6'6" when he entered the Academy. But he didn't stop there. He kept growing, and as he did, so did his game. Suddenly, from just another gangly kid with no particular standout skills, he developed into a factor on the court, a strapping center pushing 7'0", who could set up underneath and not get moved out easily.

Perhaps the turning point came in a low profile tournament in Carbondale, Illinois, quaintly called the Saluki Shootout. Playing against Southern Illinois and Western Illinois, Robinson blasted off, scoring 68 points and grabbing 31 rebounds. "It was pretty incredible," he said. "It was the first time I got an idea of what I could do."

From out of nowhere, Robinson had arrived. He blossomed into a big-time player, averaging 23.6 points and 11.6 rebounds per game. If there was a complaint with his game it was that he often seemed too laid-back, not fired-up enough about this business of basketball.

That summer, Robinson was selected for the U.S. National team that would play in the Jones Cup competition at Barcelona. Future pros like Chuck Person, Dell Curry, and Larry Krystkowiak were on the squad, all dashing around with little concern for life or limb. Robinson decided that would not be his approach. "I was thinking, 'No way I'm going to dive on the floor,'" he said.

The next thing he knew, there was his roommate, Krystkowiak, sprawled out on two banged-up knees, going after a loose ball. "I looked at Larry and he was rolling around all hurt," Robinson said. "I thought, 'Who am I not to be making an effort because I'm not even as good as these guys?' From that point on, I started working harder. That was probably one of the biggest changes in my life."

Robinson's sudden evolution into a big-time college player got him thinking about a transfer from Navy to a place where his skills would get more of a national showcase and perhaps be honed more completely toward a possible future in the pros. The Naval Academy has not been an assembly line for great athletes. Except for annual games against Army, sports is strictly secondary at Annapolis. The Academy produces officers and gentlemen, not jocks.

The Navy had produced one outstanding pro athlete—Roger Staubach. Staubach won the Heisman trophy in 1963, college football's highest honor, and was drafted by the Dallas Cowboys. But Staubach could not join the team for five years; first he had to serve out Navy's post-graduation service commitment. Once he joined

At the 1986 World Championship in Madrid, Spain, Arvidas Sabonis of the Soviet team fell back, hoping the referees would call a charge on Robinson.

the Cowboys, however, he showed that the wait had been worth it. His inspired play led Dallas to great playoff success and to becoming known as "America's Team."

Staubach was the only athlete who had devoted five years to other obligations and then successfully switched to pro sports. Could Robinson let his skills deteriorate for five years and then hope to make it in the ultra-elite world of pro basketball?

"Basically, I was scared," Robinson candidly admitted. But then he wondered, "Where would I go? Would I be comfortable? What if I transfer somewhere and then (somebody bigger than me) comes along?"

Given that Robinson was happy at Navy—happy with his courses in esoteric academic areas such as data structures, weapons and systems engineering, economic geography, math modeling, and celestial engineering, and happy with his low-key life there—he did not think long about leaving.

"Basketball is just something else to do, another facet of life," he said. "I'm going to be a success at whatever I choose. The Academy prepares me to be that."

With Robinson in place, Navy became something more than a cream puff opponent. In his junior year, the Middies were a major team. Robinson averaged 22.7 points and 13 rebounds per game and Navy battled its way into the 64-team postseason NCAA tournament, a place where service academies are rarely found.

In their first-round game, the Middies had an unusually daunting task of facing Syracuse University in the cavernous Carrier Dome, a place where basketball crowds of 30,000 or more are routine. Supposedly, teams do not play on home courts during the tournament, although curiously the University of Kansas somehow keeps ending up playing in Kemper Arena in Kansas City, a cozy 40 miles or so from its campus in Lawrence. But the Syracuse affair was even more outrageous. The Carrier Dome isn't 40 miles from campus. It's right there, smack in the middle of the upstate New York campus. That arrangement gave a rather substantial home court advantage to the Orangemen, a powerhouse team used to strong opposition and postseason play.

Playing five against 30,000 is no fun, but Robinson had a picnic against Syracuse. He scored 35 points, 26 of them in the second half setting a Carrier Dome record, and tied an NCAA tournament record with 27 free throws. Although the Orangemen were only one year away from a Final Four trip, they simply couldn't handle Robinson and were knocked out of the tournament in the opening round, right there in their own building. And the man responsible was Robinson. "He's the best," said Syracuse's Dwayne "Pearl" Washington, "He's more dangerous than (Patrick) Ewing because he's better on offense."

Navy next played Cleveland State, which had done its own giant-killing act by knocking off Indiana University in the NCAA opener. Robinson was on a roll. He blocked a record nine shots in that game and the Middies won again.

Navy then lost to a strong team from Duke University. Robinson was livid. He figured his team, not the Blue Devils, should have been in Dallas, playing Louisville for the national championship.

The next summer, Robinson played on the United States team in the world championships. The final came down to a classic good guy vs. bad guy showdown between the USA and the Soviet Union.

Robinson was matched against veteran center Arvidas Sabonis, who outweighed Robinson by 30 pounds and was two inches taller to boot.

But Robinson was superb. He outscored Sabonis 20-16 and outplayed him at both ends of the court down the stretch as the Americans won the gold medal.

"I did get a chance to play against big, strong guys on this trip and it helped me in many ways," he said. "Because they get away with so much physical stuff, you have to make a much stronger move to the basket. It's a different game. You have to think differently. It was a tougher game."

And Robinson came back a tougher player. He had added inches to his size and now he was adding intensity to his psyche. This was becoming quite a basketball package. And, by the way, the Navy had noticed.

At 7'1", there was no way Robinson could fit comfortably in a plane or ship. He was simply too tall. If he had not been a basketball player, he probably would have been patted on the back and sent on his way, unfit for service. But he was a high-profile case, one the country was focusing on.

Midway through his senior year, the Pentagon decided to reduce Robinson's postgraduation commitment to two years. Of course, if David happened to spend part of the hitch playing for the United States in the 1987 Pan Am Games and 1988 Olympics, why the Navy would certainly understand.

Robinson was not sure how to react to the decision when Navy secretary John H. Lehman made this announcement. Although he had been ambivalent about pro basketball before, now Robinson was anxious to play in the NBA. He had considered a part-time Navy, part-time NBA arrangement, much like the authorities had per-

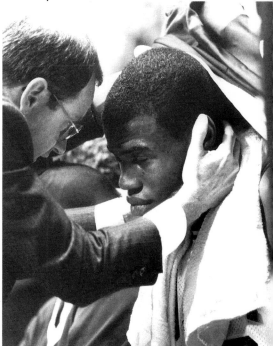

Coach Pete Herrmann tries to congratulate Robinson, who had just set a Navy record by scoring 50 points. Robinson, named winner of the annual Naismith Award earlier that day, was not happy because the University of Michigan still won the 1987 NCAA playoff game.

At the graduation ceremony at Annapolis, David Robinson got to shake the hand of Vice President George Bush.

mitted ex-Navy running back Napoleon McCallum to pursue with the NFL's Los Angeles Raiders.

"We talk a lot," Robinson said of himself and McCallum. "For Napoleon, it has been real hard. Practicing all the time, working in the Navy, putting the two together have been real tough for him. He told me the money I'll be offered will be attractive but that I should be careful and live day to day. There will always be a need (in the pros) for a big man. I'll still be seven feet tall in two years."

If nothing else, Robinson was a realist about his situation. "As far as the Navy getting something out of me," he said, "it would get more out of me playing basketball than it would if I was sitting behind some desk in some room with nobody thinking about me.

"I am positive publicity for the Navy and I can see the Navy benefiting from that. And I can understand serving my commitment in a way that people wouldn't conventionally think of."

Most scouts felt Robinson was a can't-miss player and his credentials were substantial. Consider the numbers from his senior year at Navy. He averaged 28.2 points, 11.8 rebounds, and 4.50 blocks per game. He also had the ability to do what Navy needed to win. In one game against James Madison, the Middies trailed with time running out. In a desperation play, Robinson made a remarkable catch of a sailing inbounds pass, whirled and in one motion drilled a line-drive three-pointer from 40 feet away that rattled into the net and won the game. It was the only three-pointer he ever attempted in four years at the Academy and one of the shots he remembers best.

In his final season, Robinson led the NCAA in blocks, was third in scoring, and fourth in rebounding and was the Player of the Year, sweeping all the postseason awards, including the Naismith and Wooden. He was a unanimous All-America choice and ended his collegiate career with an exclamation point by scoring 50 points in his final game against the University of Michigan, the most by any player in an NCAA tournament game since 1971. The final totals were stunning: 33 school records, 2,669 points, 1,314 rebounds, and a 61.3 shooting percentage.

He finished at Navy as the first player in NCAA history to combine over 2,500 points and 1,300 rebounds and shoot better than 60 percent. He set NCAA records for blocked shots in a career (516), a season (207), and a game (14).

"I can't even describe how much I've grown and broadened as a player and a person in the last four years," he said. "The reason for that has been the Academy."

On May 20, 1987, the Naval Academy conducted its graduation ceremonies. Among the newly commissioned officers was Midshipman First Class David M. Robinson, assigned to the civil engineer corps on a restricted list billet. The designation limited Midshipman Robinson's duty because of his size.

This, however, would not be a problem for the NBA. The league where they play for pay absolutely loved his size.

3

AN OFFICER AND A GENTLEMAN

Bad teams in the NBA have one thing going for them—they get first crack at the best talent coming out of college. When it occurred to the proprietors of the NBA that poor teams might be tempted to lose games at season's end intentionally to insure themselves of the number one pick in the draft, they developed a draft lottery, which gave the worst teams a shot at the best college player.

Patrick Ewing was the first lottery pick in 1985, drafted by the New York Knicks. The next year, the Cleveland Cavaliers used their number one pick to select Brad Daugherty. Basketball theory at the time held that a team had to have a big man in the middle in order to compete.

In 1987, David Robinson was the best big man in college basketball and it was clear that he

On the morning of the 1987 NBA draft, David Robinson was having fun with his brother Chuck at the White House after visiting Vice President Bush and watching President Ronald Reagan depart by helicopter for a trip to Florida.

should be the top player drafted. But would the team with the first pick be willing to wait while Robinson devoted the next two years of his life to the U.S. Navy?

Seven teams were in the lottery that year — the Los Angeles Clippers with the league's worst record at 12-70, New York and New Jersey, both 24-58, San Antonio (28-54), Sacramento (29-53), Cleveland (31-51), and Phoenix (36-46). The Knicks and Cleveland already had their big men in place with Ewing and Daugherty. The other five openly admitted their desire to draft Robinson, his Naval obligation notwithstanding.

Robinson had talked vaguely of preferring the Boston Celtics or Los Angeles Lakers, both perennial NBA powers, for his next basketball stop. He had options. He could sign with the team that drafted him and maintain his amateur status during his Navy hitch. Or he could play it cool and wait two years before re-entering the draft, by which time the Celtics or Lakers might be in the lottery. Or he could wait a year beyond that and become a free agent, available to the highest bidder. "It's great to have options," Robinson said.

On lottery day, the San Antonio Spurs got lucky and captured the number one pick. The first question to Bob Bass, who represented the Spurs at the lottery, after he came away with the top pick, was whether San Antonio would be willing to wait two years for Robinson. Bass laughed. "We've waited 14 years," he said. "We can wait two more."

In this obviously posed picture, the Navy shows off its biggest guns—the forecastle of the battleship USS Iowa and David Robinson.

The Spurs were a terrible team, last in the Midwest Division, and next to last in the league in attendance. Writers compared the team to the defenders of the Alamo, as each found themselves outgunned and surrounded by hostile forces. The right to draft the best player in college basketball was the first good thing that had happened to the franchise in years.

Ensign David Robinson, intrigued by the prospects of turning around a sad sack team — he had experience in doing that from his days at the Naval Academy — had other matters to deal with first. He was due at the Trident submarine base in Kings Bay, Georgia, by July 6, 1987, to begin his active duty service.

Assignment: Assistant Resident Officer in Charge of Construction. Salary: $315.23 per month. Welcome to the Navy, Mr. Robinson.

Robinson tried to fit in like just another sailor assigned to the construction of the new Kings Bay facility, even though he was hardly that. While San Antonio was anxious to get some word, some small indication of encouragement from him, Robinson said nothing, preferring to concentrate on his duties as an officer and a gentleman. "I'm in a pretty good situation," he said. "I can wait. There's no reason to rush into anything. I just want to relax and enjoy my experience in the Navy."

It's not like he was going to be away from the game. Two weeks into his assignment in Georgia, he was off to Louisville to practice with the U.S. team for the Pan American Games. A month later, he was in Indianapolis for the competition. The Navy, which had barred any part-time pro arrangement for Robinson, routinely allows time off for international competition.

Robinson and future pro teammate J. R. Reid celebrate after winning the bronze medal in the 1988 Olympics, defeating Australia 78-49.

Coach Denny Crum of Louisville assembled a strong Pan Am team and the U.S. team Americans cruised through the tournament until the gold medal game when Robinson had 20 points and 10 rebounds before fouling out with just over six minutes to play. Brazil went on to end America's 34-game Pan Am winning streak, defeating the U.S. 120-115.

After the Pan Am disappointment, Robinson went to visit San Antonio to see if he would like playing and living there. The town was so excited it planned a parade but Robinson, a low-key individual, sent word that he'd prefer a little less hoopla. As difficult as that was for a Texas city to manage, the town chose instead a welcoming party of 700 or so fans, including the mayor and a state senator at the airport. It was like a pep rally. They chanted "Da-vid! Da-vid! Da-vid!" as he got off the plane.

There was a helicopter tour, country club hospitality, lodging at a posh hotel, lavish treatment from start to finish.

Robinson was, if not flabbergasted, certainly impressed. "Before, when people said 'What do you think about San Antonio?' I couldn't really tell them anything because I had no real picture in my mind about San Antonio," he said. "From what we've seen of this city, this is a fantastic place and we love it here. That aspect of it seems perfect. Of course, there's the basketball aspect of it, too. I have to do what's going to be right for me. I have a lot to think about. It's going to take me a while to mull over."

Robinson and his family had been impressed by their visit to San Antonio and his talks with team officials. Spurs officials convinced Robinson of their determination to turn the sorry Spurs into a competitive NBA franchise and so, in November 1987, he signed an eight-year, $26-million contract with the team. Angelo Drossos, owner of the Spurs, trumpeted Robinson's deal. "It's the biggest contract in pro sports anywhere in the world," he gushed. "There's no comparison."

Robinson made it clear that the agreement involved more than just cold, hard cash. "There is no amount of money I would have signed for if I didn't think the team had a commitment to becoming better and becoming a successful franchise," Robinson said. "Bringing me in I feel like wouldn't be enough to make a successful franchise, but there are some talented players who are going to get a lot of experience in the next few years. I feel I can come in here and make my impact and we will be successful. I'm the one who had to live with this decision and I sat down and carefully thought it out and decided this was the place I wanted to be."

Getting there would take a while, though. Robinson was still on active duty with the Navy and soon would be on active duty with the U.S. Olympic team. Even though his basketball skills were a tad rusty — sitting behind a desk at a submarine base does that to a guy, even one who's 7'1" — the selection of Robinson to the 1988 team was a no-brainer.

Olympic coach John Thompson of Georgetown University pulled together some high-powered college talent for Team USA. The roster included a fistful of talented players who would move on to productive careers in the NBA. Besides Robinson, there was Danny Manning, who had led Kansas to the NCAA championship in April, Mitch Redmond, Dan Majerle, J. R. Reid, Bimbo Coles, Willie Anderson, and Charles Smith. Somehow, though, the team seemed to lack the chemistry to be successful. Ultimately, it was not, losing in a showdown against the Soviet Union 82-76 despite 19 points and 12 rebounds by Robinson. It was his best game of an otherwise ordinary tournament in which he averaged just 12.8 points and 6.8 rebounds. The Americans took home the bronze medal, their poorest finish ever in the Olympic tournament. In part, it was a function of having American college kids playing against the pros of other nations, a condition that would change after 1988.

The Pan Am and Olympic disappointments hung heavy over Robinson. "It was real disappointing and for a long time, I blamed myself," he said. "I was a big part of both teams and we were favored to win but we didn't.

"It took a long time for me to get over it. It was especially hard for me because I had nowhere to go to forget. The other players went to the NBA or back to their colleges and could play and forget. I had to sit and think about it. I know, though, that I did the best I could."

Meanwhile, the Department of the Navy was experiencing some changes at the top. In 1987, Secretary John Lehman, who reduced Robinson's commitment from the original five years to two, was replaced by James Webb, who was followed by William Ball III. In the days after the Olympic disappointment in Seoul, with six months left on his two-year obligation, Robinson wrote Secretary Ball with a suggestion. He would be willing to add three years to his reserve obligation in exchange for an early release from active duty. Ball rejected the idea.

"I was not trying to avoid a commitment but rather to increase my commitment if the interests of the Navy could be served by such," Robinson said at the time. "I respect the secretary's decision and appreciate their time and consideration. I've enjoyed my service in the U.S. Navy and look forward to serving the remaining six months on active duty and six years of reserve duty with pride."

The San Antonio Spurs would just have to wait a little longer.

4

WELCOME TO SAN ANTONIO

During his two-year hitch in the Navy, Robinson occasionally used leave time to pop in on San Antonio and remind the town that help was on the way. The Spurs needed plenty of it, dipping from 28 wins when they drafted Robinson in 1987 to a woeful 21 as they awaited his arrival in 1989.

The Naval commitment delayed Robinson's arrival in the league just long enough to prevent him from facing Kareem Abdul-Jabbar. The closest Robinson got to Kareem was sitting on the San Antonio bench as Abdul-Jabbar began his farewell season in a game against the Spurs.

Even with Abdul-Jabbar gone, there were plenty of other big men for Robinson to face — veterans such as Moses Malone of Atlanta and Robert Parish of Boston, younger stars such as Hakeem Olajuwon of Houston and Patrick Ewing of New York. The Spurs kept Robinson busy in

Before getting to play in the NBA, Robinson shows off his form in the Vince Lombardi charity golf tournament.

Once Robinson joined the NBA, he made his presence known immediately—and started rivalries against all the leading centers, including Hakeem Olajuwon.

the summer leagues, hoping that concentrated action would help rub off two years of rust. It seemed to work. Robinson dominated games against other rookies and free agents, a tower of strength under the basket. His pro debut was an intrasquad game in which he produced a triple double — 31 points, 17 rebounds, and 10 blocks. Management could not contain its enthusiasm. "He shocked all of us," assistant coach Alvin Gentry said. "I kept hearing how teams like Dallas lost their center for 40 games," said club official Bob Bass. "We lost ours for 164."

The Spurs team Robinson joined was dramatically different. San Antonio had cleaned house from the previous season's 21-61 team, trading for All-Star Terry Cummings and veteran guard Mo Cheeks, and drafting All-American Sean Elliott. The reconstruction of the Spurs had begun with a new center as the centerpiece.

Robinson tried to downplay his impact. "I have to go and play Ewing and Olajuwon and those guys," he said. "I'm definitely not ready for that yet. I have to get my offensive skills together. It will come together, though. When the season starts, I definitely will be ready."

In an exhibition game against Parish and the Celtics, Robinson hit 10 of 16 shots for 22 points in just 23 minutes. Then he got an earful from coach Larry Brown. "I told him his game's got to start with rebounding and defense," Brown said. "We can't have him taking jump shots. We have other guys to do that."

For his part, Robinson was anxious to learn. "The coaches have been very specific, very straightforward," he said. "They tell me when I stink. My role is clearly defined, but all this is brand new to me."

The good part was that Robinson was like a sponge, anxious to soak up knowledge and apply it. He was a coach's dream, bright and equipped with outstanding natural ability. "He has been waiting a long time for this," Brown said. "He's going to be great. There's no question in my mind. He is a special player."

On Opening Night, Magic Johnson confirmed that. A year after he sat on the bench in civilian clothes and watched the Lakers beat the Spurs, Robinson was in the starting lineup for the Spurs opener against Los Angeles. He put on some show, scoring 23 points and grabbing 12 rebounds. His only block came against Johnson and it left the mercurial Magic man most impressed.

"It's hard to say he's a rookie because he's a man," Johnson explained. "Some rookies are just never rookies. Robinson's one of them."

Johnson's Laker teammate, Michael Cooper, considered Robinson's debut and said simply "David Robinson is a glass-eater."

"He's simply a great player," Coach Pat Riley said. "He's a presence and they haven't had that before."

As the season went on, Robinson fit in immediately. "I don't have individual goals," he said. "I just want us to be successful. I didn't expect to feel this comfortable this quickly. That's what surprised me the most. I come out and feel relaxed. In fact, sometimes, I'm too relaxed. I've got to get out there and be a little more reckless."

Cummings thought he knew the reason for that. "David doesn't know how good he is yet," he said. "He's so good that most people aren't good enough to even push him so he has a tendency at times not to push himself."

There were inevitable showdowns with the league's quality centers, guys like Olajuwon and Ewing, and each time Robinson held his own. Around the league, he was gaining respect game by game. He was a load under the basket and he could run the court probably better than any other big man in the league. He was the full package. Game after game, Robinson put up huge numbers. There was a 21-rebound game against Chicago, a 12-block game against Minnesota, and a 41-point game against Golden State. He was the only rookie selected for the All-Star Game and when he finished the season averaging 24.3 points and 12 rebounds per game, he was the unanimous choice for NBA Rookie of the Year.

The arrival of Robinson had a huge impact on the Spurs. The team accomplished the greatest single season turnaround in NBA history. In 1988-89, the Spurs won only 21 games and finished fifth in their division. The next year, they won 56 games and finished in first place.

In 1992, (left to right) Darryl Green, defensive back of the Washington Redskins, Barry Sanders, running back of the Detroit Lions, David Robinson, and A. C. Green, forward of the Los Angeles Lakers, joined together in song. The leading members of the Athletes for Abstinence recorded the tune "It Ain't Worth It" to help young people make right choices in their sexual behavior.

In between tearing up the league, Robinson, already an accomplished self-taught musician, took up song writing. The Renaissance man is always looking for new challenges.

"When David was growing up," coach Larry Brown said, "he didn't know if he wanted to be Mozart, Thomas Edison, or sing with Bon Jovi. He's finally made the decision to become a great basketball player."

Athletes are usually judged by how good their most recent performance was. It is not enough to do great things for one game, one week, one month, or even one season. They have to prove they can perform with consistency, showing that they are not a flash in the pan, or a one-time wonder. David Robinson proved that in his second NBA season.

Robinson continued to be the wheelhouse of the Spurs operation, averaging 25.6 points with a 55.2 field goal percentage, 13 rebounds, 3.90 blocks, 2.5 assists, and 1.55 steals. He was the only player in the league to be among the top 10 in four categories — first in rebounding, second in blocks, ninth in scoring, and ninth in field-goal percentage.

He had become not only a big scorer but a demon on defense. "They needed me to score all the time at Navy," he said. "Here, we need a defensive presence in the middle and that's what I've got to give them."

Working against the best big men in basketball, Robinson held up defensively. He was a second team All-Defensive choice in his rookie year and first team the next season.

The comparisons with other big men were inevitable. Particularly intriguing were the matchups when San Antonio and Robinson played Houston and Olajuwon. "Both guys are great leapers and great scorers," Houston coach Don Chaney said. "Each carries his team on his shoulders. The similarities are there. That's why everybody gets excited when they go head-to-head."

Then there were the confrontations with New York and Ewing. "I hate to see David compared to Patrick because they are different," Spurs coach Larry Brown said. "Patrick was exposed to more in college (playing in the Big East Conference) than David. David played a lot of games against Bucknell."

By his third season, Robinson had answered all the questions. He was a consistent performer, an NBA star. He became just the third player in league history to be among the top 10 in five categories. He was eighth in scoring (23.2), fourth in rebounding (12.2), first in blocks (4.49), fifth in steals (2.32), and sixth in field goal percentage (55.1). The only others to accomplish that were Cliff Hagen in 1959-60 and Larry Bird in 1985-86. Hagen is in the Hall of Fame and Bird is headed there.

What made Robinson so good then and so good now is the ability to run the floor more fluidly and with more speed than most men his size. "He's different from any other center," Larry Brown said. "He has unbelievable speed. I've seen him dribble the length of the court as if he were a guard."

It was defense, however, that made Robinson special, almost like another Bill Russell. What's more, it kept him locked in. "Scoring doesn't matter," he said. "Defense is what interests me."

Robinson was the first player in NBA history to be among the top five in rebounding, blocks, and steals and was voted Defensive Player of the Year.

The banner season ended with some disappointment, though.

A torn ligament in his left thumb forced him out of San Antonio's lineup for the final 14 games of the season. Without him, the Spurs drifted to a 5-9 finish, dropping eight games back of Utah to finish second in the Midwest Division and were swept by Phoenix in the opening round of the playoffs.

If they didn't already know, it was stark proof of just how much Mr. Robinson meant to the Spurs' neighborhood.

5
BACK TO
THE OLYMPICS

Because America had enjoyed unparalleled basketball success in international settings — the only loss was a controversial one to the Soviet Union in the gold medal game of the 1972 Olympics — Uncle Sam got a bit out of sorts over first losing the Pan Am Games basketball tournament to Brazil in 1987 and then finishing third in the 1988 Seoul Olympics after losing to Russia in the semifinals.

In 1989, with some understandable encouragement from the United States, the International Basketball Federation changed its rules. By a 56-13 vote, it decided the Olympics would be an "open competition," permitting pros to participate. America then would gather the country's very best players, plucked from the NBA to represent the nation at Barcelona in 1992.

A crowd of over 110,000 people watched David Robinson and Earvin "Magic" Johnson (to Robinson's left) march along with their fellow competitors at the Opening Day ceremonies of the 1992 Olympics.

Croatia was the only team to give the "Dream Team" any type of game. But Toni Kukoc could not get past Robinson, as Charles Barkley and Magic Johnson look on.

One by one, they were assembled, a basketball Dream Team. Imagine Magic Johnson and Michael Jordan in the same backcourt with John Stockton and Clyde Drexler to back them up. Imagine Karl Malone, Scottie Pippen, Charles

Barkley, Larry Bird, and Chris Mullin up front, with Christian Laettner, representing college players, along for the ride. At center, the Dream Team had Patrick Ewing and David Robinson.

Robinson came to Barcelona with fire in his eyes. He was the only Dream Team player who had played for the losing American squad at Seoul. It was going to be payback time for him. "It's not often when you get a second chance at a gold medal," Robinson said. "When they said NBA players would be used in '92, I didn't know what the selection process would be. I just knew that I wanted to be part of it."

The selection process was simple. The best of the best would go and Robinson fit the profile. It would be an opportunity to get even for Seoul, even though Robinson insisted revenge was not a factor with him. Still there was hurt that needed healing.

"We had been expected to win," Robinson said, "and we had been playing so well until that game against the Soviets. Then nothing went right. It definitely took me a long, long time to get over it. It was awful. I don't ever want to feel like that again."

That would not be a problem, not with this bunch. It was clear during training camp in Monte Carlo that these Americans were simply too good for the rest of the world. And Robinson had a picnic. It's not tough to get comfortable in the French Riviera playing with the best players in the world.

Right away, Robinson knew he had come to the right place.

"The guys are making me run the floor every play, because when you do that, there is a layup waiting at the other end. They are giving me the ball on the dead run and they expect you to catch it and put it away. I'm loving this.

"Those guys reward you," he continued. "Out here, I know I'm going to get the ball when I get out and run the court. This is fun for me. It's great stuff."

For the best running center in basketball, this was like a trip to paradise.

When they got to Spain, the Dream Teamers were like the Pied Pipers of the Olympics, followed everywhere, drawing oohs and aahs from the people in the streets. It was as if the fans knew something special was about to happen and, indeed, it did.

Team USA destroyed the competition, sweeping eight games, never scoring less than 103 points, never winning by fewer than 32. Typical was a 127-83 pasting of Brazil, administered with perhaps a little more zest because of the loss to that country in the Pan Am Games in 1987. Brazilian star Oscar Schmidt used a recording studio explanation for Team USA's dominance. "They play at 33 (rpm)," he said. "We play at 45."

Was the United States playing the role of the basketball bully, beating up on little guys? Robinson, skeptical at first about using pros in the Olympics, turned vehement on that subject as the Dream Team experience went on. "If you've got the best players in the world," he said, "send the best players in the world."

Surrounded by that cast, Robinson's contributions were somewhat limited. He averaged nine points and 4.1 rebounds per game, had 12 blocks, and 14 steals. He scored 11 against Brazil, 14 against Puerto Rico, and 13 against Lithuania.

And he took home a gold medal.

For those who watched the Dream Team play, it was like textbook basketball, an awesome display of the game. "You will see professionals in the Olympics again," Team USA coach Chuck Daly said. "But I don't think you'll see a team quite like this. This was a majestic team."

6
GROWING INTO THE BEST

The Dream Team experience made an enormous impact on David Robinson. Except, perhaps, for Christian Laettner, just out of college at the time, Robinson was the lowest profile player of the team. "He says nothing," chuckled Larry Bird, "and he gets a lot of grief."

The lead needler was Charles Barkley, considered a world champion in the art. "We wouldn't be here at all if it wasn't for you," Barkley teased Robinson. "If you had won the gold, no way people would care about sending us."

Robinson took the teasing good-naturedly. And he took some other things, too, like an understanding of what leadership can mean to a basketball team. That lesson came from Magic Johnson. "You learn a lot by watching other guys and seeing what's going on," Robinson said. "The way Magic with all his experience has kind of grabbed the team. Just watching these guys is showing me that I have a lot to learn.

The Admiral goes in for a slam dunk as a beaten Shaquille O'Neal can only watch.

He did some teaching, too, though. "A lot of guys (on the Olympic team) have a tremendous ability to focus on basketball and that heightens my intensity, which is good," he said. "I try to give them a different look at life, a larger picture. We don't live on this earth just to play ball and put a lot trophies on our shelf."

Robinson's NBA apprenticeship was over. He was now an established star, preparing to play for his third pro coach. Larry Brown had been replaced by Bob Bass midway through the 1991-92 season and then the Spurs imported college coach Jerry Tarkanian for 1992-93. That move seemed doomed almost immediately as the Spurs began the season looking disorganized. The Tarkanian adventure was short-lived. After a 9-11 start, he was fired, replaced by John Lucas. Robinson was beginning to feel like he was caught in a revolving door of bench bosses.

People around the league recognized Robinson was now an elite center. Comparisons with contemporaries Ewing and Olajuwon were less frequent. He was younger than both of them and faster than either of them. He had become the Spurs' tower of power, a defensive force and explosive on offense.

With the low-key Lucas on the sidelines instead of the frenetic Tarkanian, the Spurs took off, winning 24 of their next 28 games. Robinson flourished. He was the only player on the roster to start all 82 games, leading the team in scoring 44 times, in rebounding 63 times, in blocks 68 times, and in steals 34 times.

He scored in double figures in 81 of the season's 82 games, hitting 20 points or more 54 times. He had a 52-point game against Charlotte and a 21-rebound game against Philadelphia. There were times when he was simply unstoppable.

Robinson now had the ability to control games. Asked if any player gave him a difficult time, he smiled shyly. "No, not really," he said. "One on one, there really isn't anybody. Some teams are better than others at rotating and helping and that is what gives me problems, just like any other post player. I happen to have a good mix between quickness and power.

"I have played against a lot of players who were bigger than me, but not necessarily stronger than me, and I have to have good strength and balance," he continued. "I really don't think that there is one person in particular who is going to give me a real tough time on a given night."

And that would include all of the usual suspects — Olajuwon, Ewing, and the new hotshot in Orlando, Shaquille O'Neal.

There was some alarm around the Spurs when Robinson became a born-again Christian. The concern was that his zest for religion might reduce his zeal for basketball. Robinson put that to rest in a hurry. "God doesn't want any wimps," he said.

Off the court, he formed the David Robinson Foundation and donated more than $500,000 to programs addressing the physical and spiritual needs of the family. On the court, he remained the essential member of the Spurs franchise.

And then a strange thing happened to him. Overnight, one of the best rebounders in the NBA became the second best rebounder on the Spurs. That was because San Antonio traded for the best board man in the league, enigmatic Dennis Rodman.

Coach John Lucas helped instruct David Robinson and make the Spurs a top contender in the NBA.

Covered with tattoos and dying his hair a different color of the rainbow every night, Rodman settled into San Antonio and quickly formed a relationship with Robinson. They became basketball's odd couple, the straight-laced Robinson on a blistering scoring pace and the march-to-his-own-drummer Rodman pulling down rebound after rebound.

They made commercials together including one pizza ad in which the buttoned-down Robinson advised Rodman to loosen up. Rodman, of course, was already as loose as they come.

On the court, Coach Lucas surrounded them with role players, bounced out the basketball, and let them play. And the Spurs went on a tear, winning 25 of 29 games over one stretch. Robinson soared to the top of the scoring race and got into the game-by-game duel for the lead with O'Neal that did not end until the season's final game. Rodman egged him on with rebounding resolve and occasionally some far-out behavior, such as sitting with courtside fans instead on the bench after coming out of a game.

"We're an odd collection of people," Robinson said, considering the Spurs roster. "But the thing is these guys genuinely root for each other. We're not the most talented team but we use that talent to play with a lot of enthusiasm."

Robinson flourished in the odd mix. He scored 50 points in one game against Minnesota, 46 in another against Boston. In one game against Detroit, he achieved the rarest of NBA feats — a quadruple double. He reached double figures in four categories: 34 points, 10 rebounds, 10 assists, and 10 blocks. It was just the fourth time it had happened in NBA history and some of the greatest players in the history of the league—Jordan, Johnson, Chamberlain, Bird, and Abdul-Jabbar—had never managed it. The only others to achieve it were Nate Thurmond, Alvin Robertson, and Robinson's old pal, Hakeem Olajuwon.

Robinson admitted that the addition of Rodman had a profound effect on his game. "Dennis brings a different kind of fire to the game, a fire you can't help but feel," Robinson said. "I was too much of a gentleman; he was too wild. The best way I can describe it is I don't feel like I'm going into battle unarmed anymore."

Robinson won the scoring title at 29.8 points per game and Rodman led the league in rebounding with 17.3 — the first time in NBA history that teammates had won those two titles. Robinson was the first center to lead the league in scoring since Bob McAdoo in 1975-76. He also finished second in the MVP race to Olajuwon and some people thought the award had gone to the wrong guy. Rodman was one of them.

"David is the MVP," he said. "I'll take second runner-up."

With all the success of the regular season, the Spurs again came up short in the playoffs, losing in the first round to Utah. The failure cost Lucas his job. For 1994, San Antonio hired Bob Hill as the new coach — the fifth bench boss for Robinson.

The arrival of a new coach did not change an awful lot for the man in the middle except for one thing. Coming that close to the MVP title made him a man with a mission, a man determined to put another trophy on his own shelf.

7

MVP AND A
SPUR FOREVER

David Robinson came into the 1994-95 NBA season with a list of accomplishments that bordered on awesome. In five seasons he had been Rookie of the Year, led the league in rebounding, been named Defensive Player of the Year, led the league in blocked shots, and won a scoring championship.

He had scored 71 points in a game and had 24 rebounds in two others. He had 11 assists in a game and 12 blocks in another. Twice he had six steals in a game.

He would not reach any of those plateaus in his sixth season. Although he did not lead the league in any category, it turned out to be his best season yet.

In 1994-95, the Spurs put together the best record in the league at 62-20. Robinson was their best player. His statistics remained consistently outstanding. He scored in double figures in all 82 games with 20 or more points 68 times,

Robinson keeps his eyes on the ball—and his sights on an NBA championship.

and 30 or more 36 times. Six times he blistered opponents for 40 or more points. He had a season-high 43 points against the Dallas Mavericks on January 15 and scored 42 four times and 40 once. In 52 games he scored in double figures and also was in double figures for rebounds, blocks, or assists.

He was among the league leaders in five categories — third in scoring (27.6), fourth in blocks (3.23), seventh in rebounds (10.8), 15th in steals (1.65), and 15th in field-goal percentage (.530). He led in only one department — voting for the Most Valuable Player award.

Robinson received 73 of a possible 105 first place votes and easily outdistanced Shaquille O'Neal for the MVP award. Karl Malone was third and Patrick Ewing fourth. It was Robinson's time and everybody seemed to know it. There was no argument with the vote. "If he didn't win it," teammate Sean Elliott said, "the NBA would have the legitimacy of a Don King production."

For Robinson, the MVP award was vindication of his role with the Spurs. "Carrying the team is a whole lot different than coming out and just being good every night," he said. "Being able to withstand that kind of pressure night in and night out, and not only withstand it, but excel under it, I think that's where I've been able to grow.

"When I first came into the league, I really didn't know how to play the way I play now. It's a big credit to the coaches who have taught me to push myself harder and go out and do more things on the floor every night."

Robinson learned something from each of his coaches. Larry Brown drilled him on defense. Bob Bass and Jerry Tarkanian, even in their short terms, gave him different aspects to focus on. John Lucas gave Robinson the opportunity to score at will. Bob Hill turned the Spurs over to the Admiral and taught him how to be the team leader. Robinson slowly pulled it together much like an architect working on a blueprint. The result was an NBA superstar, a perennial All-Star, one of the best players in the game.

It was not easy and for a long time, he did not have a lot of help. "At one point," he said, "I remember looking at our roster and thinking that we didn't even have anybody on the team whom anybody wanted. We didn't have anybody to trade."

Slowly, though, the Spurs imported help, often retrieving players that had been traded away previously such as Sean Elliott and Avery Johnson. Robinson appreciated the changes and the commitment to creating a competitive program.

With two years left on his original contract the Spurs decided it was time to make a new deal with Robinson. The result was a multiyear contract — the Spurs wouldn't say for how long or how much — that general manager Gregg Popovich said would keep Robinson with the team "for life."

"We're going to see a lot of David for a lot of years," Popovich said. "As long as he plays, he'll be a Spur."

That suited Robinson. "Changing uniforms wasn't of interest to me," he said. "There might have been an opportunity to maybe make a couple of more dollars somewhere else but in my career, that hasn't been the biggest driving force for me. When you are chasing the dollar it might not be in the place that you are and you might go other places to find that opportunity."

The Spurs won more games than any other team in the 1995 regular season, but Hakeem Olajuwon and the Houston Rockets defeated San Antonio in the playoffs en route to their second world championship.

That is not Robinson's style. He signed the contract in December and two months later appeared in his seventh consecutive All-Star game, this time at home in San Antonio.

The 1996 season also ended too soon for Robinson's tastes. In the second round of the playoffs, the Utah Jazz unceremoniously dumped the Spurs in six games, winning by an average of over 20 points. The Admiral had a sub-par series, often getting in foul trouble and setting a new low for scoring in one game—just 6 points.

Robinson had one major consolation, though. He also was selected for the 1996 Olympic team — the first American to play on three Olympic basketball squads.

The honors kept pouring in for the humble man who went out for basketball just to get a varsity letter at Navy. None of it meant more to him, though, than the Olympic selection.

"For me, that is fantastic," he said. "I told my wife and family that I wouldn't play anymore, that I have played in so many international tournaments that I wouldn't play. It is so different when they call and ask you if you want to play. Just the thought of playing with these guys and their level of talent is great. I remember the experiences with the first Dream Team. It was phenomenal. Practices were incredible. It was a great experience."

The 1996 Dream Team included two of Robinson's pivot pals, Shaquille O'Neal and Hakeem Olajuwon, along with Penny Hardaway, Reggie Miller, Scottie Pippen, Gary Payton, John Stockton, Karl Malone, and Grant Hill. Four of them — David Robinson, Stockton, Malone, and Pippen — were repeaters from the 1992 Dream Team. Just one, Robinson, went back to the 1988 Games. "It is just a great opportunity to play with these guys," he said. "I couldn't pass something like that up."

The 1996 Dream Teamers again brought home the gold medal at the Atlanta Olympics. They were not quite as impressive in beating their competition as earlier Dream Teams, but they got the job done.

So Robinson plays on, still excelling, still finding challenges to overcome. He is in the prime of his basketball life now, equipped with all the trappings of greatness. He would like an NBA championship to complete the picture and then he could begin thinking about life after basketball. He talks about the ministry as a possibility, about doing things to help others. And he defines himself simply.

"If I were describing myself to other people I'd say, 'He may not know everything, but boy, he really has a desire to learn.' That is the one thing that I think has been the strongest part of my game since I've been in the league. I have grown a lot and have really enjoyed the learning part. And I continue to want to get better."

STATISTICS

David Robinson

Year	Team	FGM	FGA	PCT	FTM	FTA	PCT	REB	PTS	AVG
1983-84	Navy	86	138	.493	42	73	.575	111	214	7.6
1984-85	Navy	302	469	.644	152	243	.626	370	756	23.6
1985-86	Navy	294	484	.607	208	331	.628	455	796	22.7
1986-87	Navy	350	592	.591	202	317	.637	378	903	28.2
Totals		1032	1683	.613	604	964	.627	1314	2669	21.0

Year	Team	FGM	FGA	PCT	FTM	FTA	PCT	REB	PTS	AVG
1989-90	San Antonio	690	1300	.531	613	837	.732	983	1993	24.3
1990-91	San Antonio	754	1366	.552	592	777	.762	1063	2101	25.6
1991-92	San Antonio	592	1074	.551	393	561	.701	829	1578	23.2
1992-93	San Antonio	676	1348	.488	561	766	.732	956	1916	23.4
1993-94	San Antonio	840	1658	.507	696	925	.752	855	**2383**	**29.8**
1994-95	San Antonio	788	1487	.530	656	847	.774	877	2238	25.6
1995-96	San Antonio	711	1378	.516	626	823	.761	1000	2051	25.0
Totals		5051	9611	.526	4134	5536	.747	6563	14260	25.6

FGM	field goals made
FGA	field goals attempted
PCT	percent
FTM	free throws made
FTA	free throws attempted
REB	rebounds
PTS	points
AVG	average

bold indicates league-leading statistics

DAVID ROBINSON
A CHRONOLOGY

1965   Born David Maurice Robinson, August 6, at Key West, Florida

1983   Plays his only season of high school basketball at Osbourn Park in Manassas, Virginia

1984   Enrolls in the Naval Academy and averages just 7.6 points and 4.0 rebounds in his first season

1986   Leads nation in rebounds (455) and blocked shots (207)

1987   Named college player of the year; finishes college career the first player in NCAA Division I history to collect over 2,500 points and 1,300 rebounds while shooting over 60 percent from the field; is picked first in the NBA draft by the San Antonio Spurs

1988   Plays on bronze medal U.S. Olympic team at Seoul, South Korea

1990   After completing two years of naval obligations, joins Spurs; named unanimous choice as NBA Rookie of the Year and is only rookie to play in All-Star Game

1991   Only player in NBA to finish in top ten in four categories

1992   Wins a gold medal playing with the "Dream Team" at the Olympics

1994   Leads NBA in scoring, averaging 29.8 points per game and scoring 71 in last game of season to win title

1995   Named MVP as Spurs win the most games of any NBA team

1996   Becomes the first American to play on three U.S. Olympic basketball teams

SUGGESTIONS FOR FURTHER READING

Hank Hersch, "Anchors Aweigh," *Sports Illustrated*, July 6, 1987

Curry Kirkpatrick, "Back to Olympian Heights," *Sports Illustrated*, July 4, 1988

Curry Kirkpatrick, "The Mightiest Middie," *Sports Illustrated*, November 19, 1986

Jack McCallum, "Hands On," *Sports Illustrated*, January 29, 1990

Jack McCallum, "He's the Spur of the Moment," *Sports Illustrated*, November 13, 1989

Bruce Newman, "Horn of Plenty," *Sports Illustrated*, April 22, 1991

Phil Taylor, "Spur of the Moment," *Sports Illustrated*, March 7, 1994

ABOUT THE AUTHOR

Hal Bock has written about sports for the Associated Press since 1963, covering every major event including the Olympics, World Series, Super Bowls, Kentucky Derby, Final Four, and NBA Playoffs.

Bock, a native of New York City and a journalism graduate of New York University, has won five Associated Press Sports Editors awards. He lives on Long Island with his wife, a psychologist.

INDEX

PICTURE CREDITS

AP/Wide World Photos: 2, 8, 12, 17, 20, 21, 26, 30, 34, 36, 39, 44, 48, 52, 54, 58; Courtesy of the Navy: 14, 28; George Bush Presidential Library: 24; Archive Photos: 42.